BLACK BEAUTY

by
Anna Sewell

Teacher Guide

Written by
Nomi J. Waldman

Note

The Puffin Classics edition of the book, published by the Penguin Group, ©1994, was used to prepare this guide. The page references may differ in other editions. Novel ISBN: 0-14-036684-9

Please note: Please assess the appropriateness of this book for the age level and maturity of your students prior to reading and discussing it with them.

ISBN 1-58130-851-5

Copyright infringement is a violation of Federal Law.

To order, contact your local school supply store, or—
Novel Units, Inc.
P.O. Box 97
Bulverde, TX 78163-0097

Web site: www.educyberstor.com

Lori Mammen, Editorial Director
Andrea M. Harris, Production Manager/Production Specialist
Heather Johnson, Product Development Specialist
Suzanne K. Mammen, Curriculum Specialist
Lenella Meister, Production Specialist
Vicky Rainwater, Curriculum Specialist
Jill Reed, Product Development Specialist
Nancy Smith, Product Development Specialist
Adrienne Speer, Production Specialist

Table of Contents

Skills and Strategies

Comprehension
Cause/effect, compare and contrast, correct sequence, drawing conclusions, important details, summarizing, visualizing

Literary Elements
Figures of speech, mood, story map, effects of reading, flowchart

Vocabulary
British and archaic usage, dictionary of horse-related terms, crossword puzzle, dictionary use, word mapping, synonyms

Listening/Speaking
Dramatic reading, acting

Critical Thinking
Analyzing dialogue, analyzing characters, predicting, recognizing opinions

Across the Curriculum
Art—illustrating text, designing a monument; Science—anatomy of a horse; Social Studies—researching SPCA; Writing—paragraph, dedication, riddles, crossword clues, bio-poem, scene in play form, news story, point of view

Genre: fantasy

Setting: 19th-century England

Point of View: first person

Themes: courage, strength (both physical and spiritual), dealing with sudden change, kindness vs. cruelty

Conflict: person vs. animal

Style: autobiographical

Tone: initially placid but always with a hint of harsher possibilities

Date of First Publication: 1877

Summary

Black Beauty is a horse that narrates his own life story. The story begins with his earliest recollections as a colt by his mother's side. Because he is a handsome and good-tempered horse, Black Beauty seems likely to have good experiences with his human owners. At first that is true, when he is a kind gentleman's riding horse. Then circumstances change, and he has more and more difficulties. Eventually he becomes a working horse and as such is expected to perform ever-harder labor that tires and ages him. Along the way, he encounters both kind and callous owners of all classes. A society matron thoughtlessly subjects him to cruel practices in order to force him into what is considered a "smart" stance. Later, a struggling cab driver treats him as kindly and considerately as possible. All the while, the horse patiently and bravely endures, trying his best to satisfy his owners. He undergoes a series of name changes along the way before he is finally rescued by a kind family whose groom recognizes him and restores his original name, Black Beauty.

About the Author

Anna Sewell was born in Yarmouth, England, in 1820. Her mother was an author of children's books. Crippled when she was 14, Sewell achieved some mobility by horseback riding and driving a pony and carriage. Even before this, though, she loved horses and was moved to write *Black Beauty* by the cruel treatment she observed being inflicted on horses. Sewell finished the book in 1877, but did not live to see its great success. She died in 1878. The popularity of the book with youthful readers has continued even into the 21st century, with total sales of at least 30 million copies.

Background Information

Sewell meant for *Black Beauty* to be an explicit plea for the humane treatment of horses. She is quoted as having said that by writing Black Beauty's story, she wished "to induce kindness, sympathy, and an understanding treatment of horses." Using both human and equine characters to voice her feelings, she reiterates the idea that a horse will be willing and good-natured if it is treated well from the beginning. George T. Angell, president of the American Humane Education Society, strenuously promoted the book. Because of his support, the book received wide distribution. Though she earned no more than 20 pounds (approximately $35) from it, the book accomplished what Sewell had set out to do. It led to the abolishment of the hated bearing rein and created a public awareness of the importance of the humane treatment of animals.

Since its publication, *Black Beauty* has been translated into many languages and filmed four times.

Characters

Black Beauty: narrates story of his life; sold from owner to owner, experiencing various levels of treatment

Ginger: temperamental horse at Squire and Mrs. Gordon's; has been treated unfairly most of her life

Merrylegs: good-tempered horse at Squire and Mrs. Gordon's; lives next to Black Beauty

Captain: pulls Jerry Barker's cab with Black Beauty; is hit by a brewer's dray and is badly injured

Squire and Mrs. Gordon: Black Beauty's second owners; kind masters; have to sell the horses when Mrs. Gordon becomes ill

John Manly: kind coachman for Squire and Mrs. Gordon

James Howard: gentle and pleasant stable boy for Squire and Mrs. Gordon

Joe Green: quiet, young stable boy who replaces James

Lady Anne: Black Beauty's third owner; perfect horsewoman; chose Black Beauty for her horse

Reuben Smith: left in charge of stables when York, the coachman, goes to London; has a drinking problem; is killed when he wrecks the carriage after he has been drinking

Mr. Barry: Black Beauty's fifth owner; buys him for the purpose of exercise; sells him after being cheated by two grooms he has hired

Jerry Barker: Black Beauty's sixth owner; hardworking, kind cab driver; treats Black Beauty well; sells him when he takes a new job

Mr. Thoroughgood: Black Beauty's ninth owner; buys Black Beauty to try to "make him young again"

Initiating Activities

Use one or more of the following to introduce the novel.

1. Using the Prediction Chart on pages 7–8 of this guide, ask students to make predictions about the book based on their examination of the following: the cover, first page, table of contents, and back cover. If some students have seen one of the movie versions of the book, invite them to predict how close the book will be to the version they saw. Have them keep a record of their predictions so they can check them against the actual outcome of the novel.

2. Invite students to share what they know about the way horses are trained. Initiate a discussion on whether there are right and wrong ways to train a horse. Discuss how different training methods might affect the behavior and personality of a horse or other animal.

3. Encourage students familiar with horses to describe some of the different breeds and explain how they are used for different purposes based on their build, speed, and stamina.

4. Ask students to begin the Character Attribute Web on page 9 of this guide for Black Beauty. Students can add to the web as they read.

5. Have students work in pairs to complete the "Be a Detective!" graphic on page 10 of this guide.

6. Ask students to begin the Story Map on page 11 of this guide. Students can add to the map as they read.

Vocabulary Activities

discontented (26)
defiant (39)
substantial (59)
attentive (97)

peculiarities (108)
dislodge (142)
indolent (158)
dejected (163)

thoroughfare (166)
animated (176)
gallant (179)
consequence (223)

pining (223)
compensation (229)
detain (248)
sufficiently (254)

1. Self-directed Inventory: Have students list the target words above on a separate sheet of paper. Then, using the following set of four symbols, ask them to indicate their degree of familiarity with each word:

    + = "I know it and can use it in a sentence."

    √ = "I understand it when I read it in context."

    ? = "It looks familiar to me, but I don't know what it means."

    0 = "It's completely new to me."

    Encourage students to update the symbols on their lists as they read the novel.

2. Word-Learning Graph: Assign ten of the target words above for students to become familiar with. List students' names along one axis of a graph and target words along the other axis. Invite students to quiz each other on the word meanings. Once a student can correctly give a definition of or use a target word in a complete sentence, he or she may check it off the graph. You may wish to provide students with study cards that have the target words on one side and a definition and/or sample sentence on the other.

3. Defining by Synonyms and Antonyms: Provide students with a dictionary or a thesaurus. Ask students to define a set number of target words, using the following sentences as models:

    Beseeching is a synonym of begging.

    Civil is an antonym of defiant.

4. Vocabulary Chart: Have students complete the Vocabulary Chart on page 12 of this guide, identifying each word by its function in the sentence in which it first appears.

Using Predictions

We all make predictions as we read—little guesses about what will happen next, how a conflict will be resolved, which details will be important to the plot, which details will help fill in our sense of a character. Students should be encouraged to predict, to make sensible guesses as they read the novel.

As students work on their predictions, these discussion questions can be used to guide them:
What are some of the ways to predict? What is the process of a sophisticated reader's thinking and predicting? What clues does an author give to help us make predictions? Why are some predictions more likely to be accurate than others?

Create a chart for recording predictions. This could either be an individual or class activity. As each subsequent chapter is discussed, students can review and correct their previous predictions about plot and characters as necessary.

Use the facts and ideas the author gives.

Use your own prior knowledge.

Apply any new information (i.e., from class discussion) that may cause you to change your mind.

Predictions
_____
_____
_____
_____
_____

Prediction Chart

What characters have we met so far?	What is the conflict in the story?	What are your predictions?	Why did you make these predictions?

Character Attribute Web

Directions: The attribute web below will help you gather clues the author provides about a character in the novel. Fill in the blanks with words and phrases that tell how the character acts and looks, as well as what the character thinks and feels.

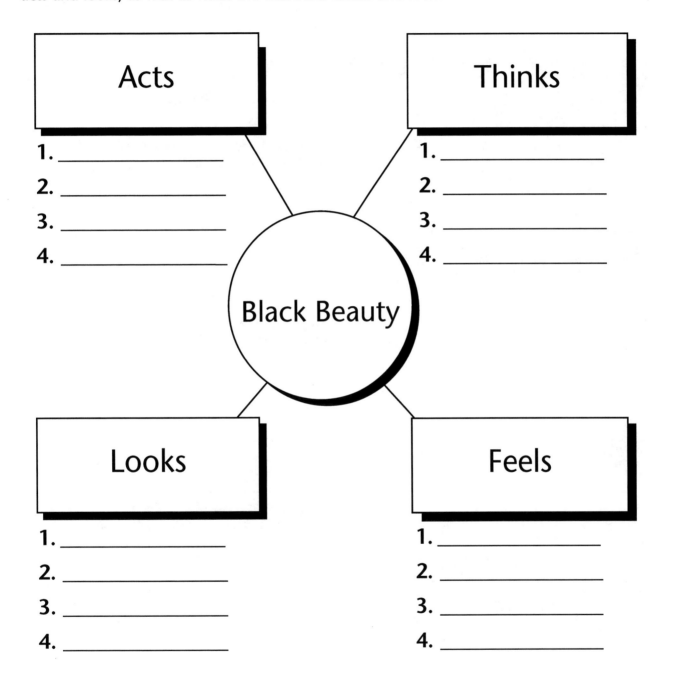

Acts

1. _____
2. _____
3. _____
4. _____

Thinks

1. _____
2. _____
3. _____
4. _____

Black Beauty

Looks

1. _____
2. _____
3. _____
4. _____

Feels

1. _____
2. _____
3. _____
4. _____

Be a Detective!

Directions: Check out the book by looking at the cover and thumbing through the pages. Then, ask yourself who, what, where, when, why, and how. Write your questions in the spaces below. Exchange papers with a partner and answer each other's questions.

Who?

_____

_____

_____

_____

When?

_____

_____

_____

_____

What?

_____

_____

_____

_____

Why?

_____

_____

_____

_____

_____

Where?

_____

_____

_____

_____

How?

_____

_____

_____

_____

_____

Story Map

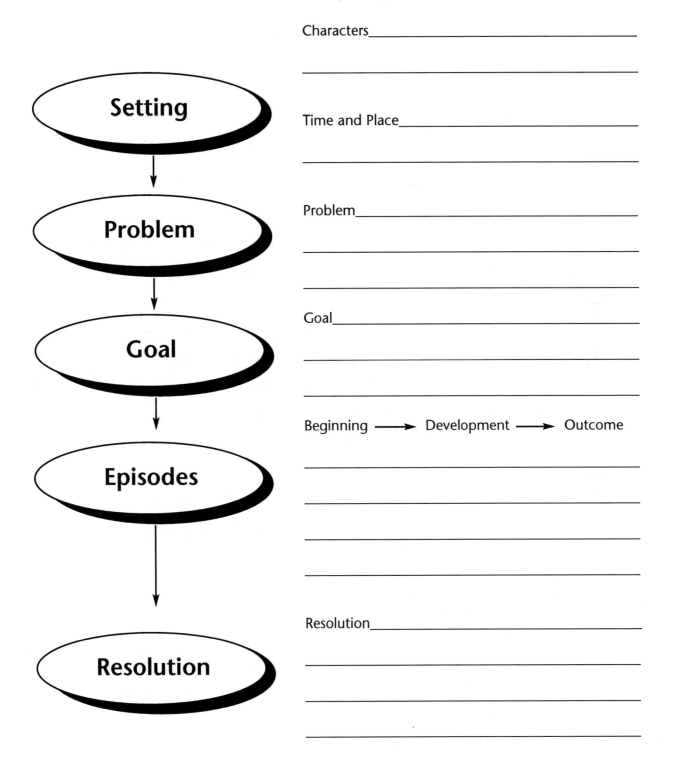

Characters_____

_____

Time and Place_____

_____

Problem_____

_____

_____

Goal_____

_____

_____

Beginning ⟶ Development ⟶ Outcome

_____

_____

_____

_____

Resolution_____

_____

_____

_____

_____

Vocabulary Chart

Noun	Verb	Adjective/Adverb	Other

Character Web

Directions: Complete the attribute web below by filling in information specific to a character in the book.

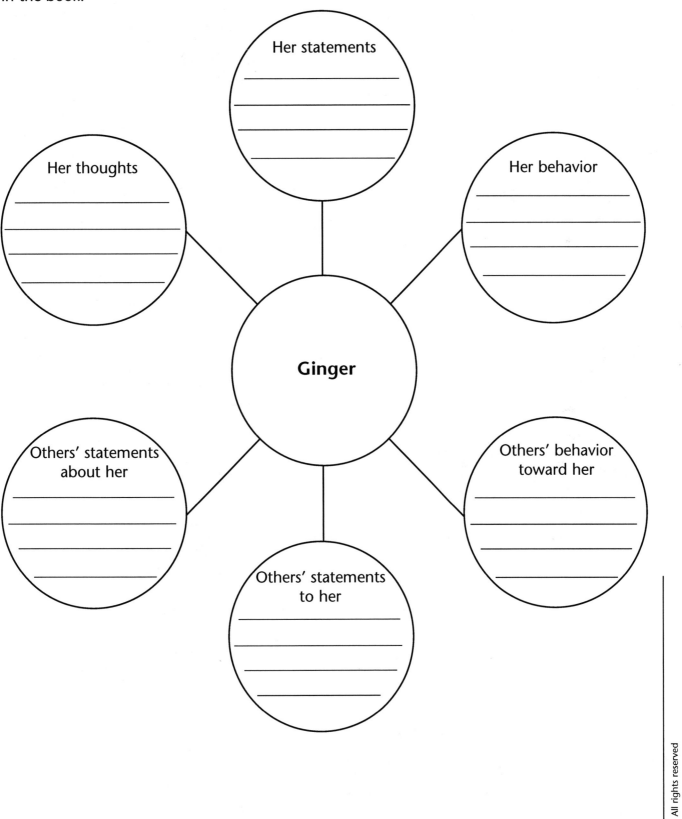

Feelings

Directions: Choose a character from the book and complete the chart below.

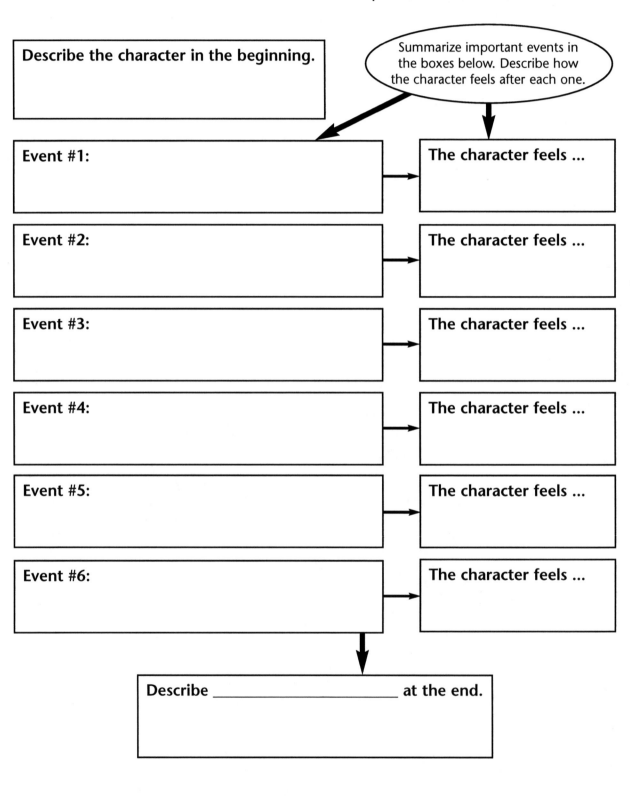

Describe the character in the beginning.

Summarize important events in the boxes below. Describe how the character feels after each one.

Event #1:

The character feels ...

Event #2:

The character feels ...

Event #3:

The character feels ...

Event #4:

The character feels ...

Event #5:

The character feels ...

Event #6:

The character feels ...

Describe _____ at the end.

Who Am I?

Directions: Write a riddle describing a character in the novel. Include adjectives, adverbs, nouns, and verbs that will help other students see this character in their mind's eye. Describe how the character looks, acts, feels, talks, and how other people in the story treat this character. (Do not reveal which character is the answer to your riddle.)

Who am I?

I have

_____

_____

_____

I can

_____

_____

_____

In the story, people say I _____

_____

_____

The Daily News

Chapters 1–9, pp. 1–45

Black Beauty, a riding horse, begins the story of his life with the time he spent with his mother, citing the advice she gave him on how to get along well with humans. He follows that advice, with mostly good results.

Vocabulary
fortnight (13)
disregard (14)
restive (14)
rook (16)
accommodation (16)
discontented (26)
skittish (27)
weaned (29)
defiant (39)

Discussion Questions

1. What advice does Black Beauty's mother give him about getting along with humans? Do you think it is good advice? Why? (*She tells him to do his best to please his master, but she also warns him that not all masters are good. Answers will vary. pp. 14–15*)

2. What was the advantage for Black Beauty of having Squire Gordon break him in? (*Squire Gordon wanted to make sure that Black Beauty's breaking in was done right and that he was not frightened or hurt. pp. 10–15*)

3. Describe the part of Black Beauty's training that he has always considered a great advantage. (*His master sent him to a meadow by a railway for a fortnight so he could get used to the sights and sounds of steam engines. pp. 13–14*)

4. Briefly summarize Ginger's story. (*Her first master did not treat her kindly. She was ill-used and worked too hard. She began kicking and biting because of a distrust of humans. She still does not fully trust anyone, even though her current master treats her well. pp. 29–40*)

5. Give two examples each from this section of the right way and wrong way to treat a horse. (*Possible examples for the right way: Squire Gordon breaks in Beauty himself without violence. [pp. 10–12] Beauty has a clean and airy stall. [p. 17] John uses the whip with a light touch. [p. 21]; Possible examples for the wrong way: The ploughboy throws things at the colts. [p. 5] Ginger's description of her forceful treatment. [pp. 30–38] Merrylegs' description of the boys who had him out too long. [pp. 41–43]*)

6. Compare and contrast Black Beauty's and Ginger's attitudes toward human beings. Explain why each horse behaves as it does. (*Beauty is treated well and, going along with his mother's advice, does his best to please his master. Ginger had a bad first experience with humans, so she finds it difficult to trust humans. Answers will vary. pp. 14–40*)

7. Evaluate the following statement by Merrylegs: "...I can tell you good places make good horses" (p. 44). Whether you agree or not, support your answer with at least two arguments. (*Students may cite Ginger's description of her first place and contrast it with Beauty's experience. Some may argue that Beauty had an easygoing disposition to begin with, while Ginger may have been more nervous. pp. 4, 29*)

Supplementary Activities

1. Word Usage: Find terms from the novel that are uniquely British or no longer commonly used, then find their definitions. Keep a record of the words on a chart or bulletin board. Examples include whilst, whence, draught, ostlers, magistrate, and coster.

2. Dictionary: Begin a loose-leaf dictionary for terms used to describe the horses and special equipment, including various horse-drawn conveyances. Examples include farrier, trot, canter, drovers, roan, cob, paddock, and chaise.

3. Literary Devices: Interpret what the author means by each of the following figures of speech:

"...my coat was brushed every day till it <u>shone like a rook's wing</u>" (p. 16).

"I <u>never had words</u> yet with horse or mare" (p. 18).

"...that will <u>show his paces</u>" (p. 21).

"...but my <u>blood was thoroughly up</u>, and I cared for nothing he could do if only I could get him off" (p. 32).

4. Point of View: Imagine that your pet, or any animal you are familiar with, could speak. Then write what you think it would say about your behavior toward it. Share your writing with a friend and discuss its accuracy as well as any reasons you see for changing your behavior.

5. Character Analysis: Complete the Character Web on page 13 of this guide for Ginger.

Chapters 10–21, pp. 46–104

Black Beauty learns more about humans' cruelty, both from Ginger's story and his own observations. He saves his owner from crossing a broken bridge in a storm and must be saved himself from a burning stable. He is separated from his kind owners when Mrs. Gordon becomes ill, and the family must leave the farm to save her life.

Vocabulary
disfigure (49)
distended (50)
substantial (59)
inclined (66)
liveries (70)
pined (87)
attentive (97)
smart (99)
determination (100)

Discussion Questions

1. Sir Oliver asks the question, "What right have they [humans] to torment and disfigure God's creatures?" (p. 49) How would you answer him if you could? *(Students may agree with him that they do not have that right, but invite them to give their own reasons for thinking that way.)*

2. How does Black Beauty save the lives of Squire Gordon and John Manly? *(He refuses to go onto a bridge during a storm. The bridge has been broken in the middle, and although his masters do not notice it, Black Beauty does. p. 61)*

3. What examples in this section show that the author's religious beliefs support her feelings about kindness to all living things? *(She refers to cruelty as being "the devil's own trade mark," meaning it is evil, while also saying "God is Love." She also refers to animals as "God's creatures." pp. 64–68)*

4. What talent does James have that enables him to rescue Black Beauty from the fire? *(He stays calm and knows to cover Beauty's eyes as he leads her out. pp. 78–79)*

5. What mistake does Joe Green make after Black Beauty returns with the Doctor? *(He gives Black Beauty a pail full of cold water and does not cover him with a cloth. pp. 91–92)*

6. How do you think Joe Green feels after his inexperience harms Black Beauty? *(He probably feels very guilty for what happened and promises himself he will do everything he can to make up for it. pp. 91–97)*

7. What caused Joe to jump "at once from a boy into a man" (p. 100)? *(He gave evidence against a man who was mistreating his horses. After that, there was more purpose and determination in all Joe did. pp. 99–100)*

Supplementary Activities

1. Writing: Write advertisements for each of the Squire's horses when the family must leave the country. Include important details that a prospective buyer would want to know, such as size, coloring, and personality. Use lively language to attract readers' attention and interest.

2. Literary Devices: Interpret what the author means by each of the following figures of speech:

   "...so I thought if I beat the bush on this side, the birds would fly out, and I should learn what I wanted to know quickly" (p. 70).

   "...I would not stand in his light for the world" (p. 71).

   "...I have top wages, and can lay by for a rainy day or a sunny day ... and Nelly is as happy as a bird" (p. 85).

3. Mood: Describe the mood at the end of Section 2. Explain how it compares to the beginning of the book.

4. Writing: Based on what you know about Black Beauty and what you have learned about the proper care of horses, state three wishes you have for how Black Beauty should be treated at his new home. Keep a record of your wishes so you can compare them with Beauty's eventual fate.

Chapters 22–31, pp. 105–160

Black Beauty is not treated well at his next home, mainly because he is required to wear the cruel bearing rein. He is repeatedly injured, through no fault of his own, and is sold to a livery stable. There he is used by a variety of people, some of whom are callous and careless. He does no better at his next home with Mr. Barry and is soon sold again.

Vocabulary

constrained (116)
interceded (126)
obliged (126)
frequented (129)
distinguish (131)
poultice (133)
foremost (136)
warrant (137)
contemptuously (143)
harassed (145)
prevailed (152)
blustered (156)

Discussion Questions

1. How do the requirements of "fashion" affect Beauty and Ginger at their new home? *(The grooms are required to use the painful and harmful bearing rein because it is supposed to make the horses look elegant. pp. 110–111)*

2. A trusting Black Beauty asks his new partner, referring to the bearing rein, "Do you think that our masters know how bad it is for us?" (p. 115) Based on Max's response, discuss where the burden of guilt lies for this mistreatment of horses. *(Students may feel that because dealers and horse doctors know the effects of the bearing rein, it is their responsibility to speak up for the horses and convince their owners to stop the practice. pp. 115–116)*

3. What are the effects of Reuben Smith's forgetting his promises to stay away from alcohol? *(Beauty is badly injured, Reuben is killed, and his family must go to the gloomy Union House. pp. 125–134)*

4. What is the fate of a job horse? What, if anything, might the owner of the horse do to change this? *(Because many different people can rent a job horse, they each treat the horse differently. There may not be too much the owner can do except perhaps offer such reminders as not to overload the horse, use the whip, go too fast, or leave it out in bad weather. pp. 139–143)*

5. How does Peggy's experience show the importance of having a well-matched pair of horses? *(Because she has a different pace due to her small size, she constantly has to strain herself to keep up with another, bigger horse. pp. 147–150)*

6. Based on the actions of the groom, Alfred Smirk, what do you think a humbug is? *(a person who pretends to be one thing but behaves differently, pp. 157–160)*

7. Why does Mr. Barry decide to sell Black Beauty? *(He is frustrated after having been deceived by two grooms. He decides to hire a horse when he wants one. p. 160)*

Supplementary Activities

1. Research: Make a list of the various remedies that were used on Black Beauty and other horses. Research modern veterinary medicines to find what remedies are used today. How are veterinary medicines like those used on humans?

2. Social Studies: Research the origin of the Society for the Prevention of Cruelty to Animals (SPCA) and report on it.

3. Creative Writing: Imagine that you are an inspector for the SPCA. You have been asked to investigate one of the incidents Beauty describes in this part of the novel. Choose an incident and reread it. Then create a report of the incident such as an inspector might write.

4. Art: Brainstorm ways in which horses are used in today's world. Prepare an illustrated chart that lists each activity and gives a brief description of the activity.

5. Writing: Imagine that Black Beauty has omitted a paragraph at the end of Part 2 in which he describes his feelings about being sold again. Write the "missing" paragraph for him.

Chapters 32–45, pp. 161–242

Sold at a horse fair, Beauty is lucky enough to be purchased by a kind cab driver, Jerry Barker. While transporting passengers around the city, Beauty witnesses other horses being treated harshly, including his old friend Ginger. When the cabman's health fails, Black Beauty is sold again.

Vocabulary

palisades (171)
caparisoned (176)
champing (177)
gallant (179)
portmanteau (183)
earnestly (183)
obliging (184)
constitution (226)
vexation (229)
consultations (239)

Discussion Questions

1. How do you feel about the scenes Captain describes? Do you think it is right to use animals in the wars that human beings fight? Explain. *(Some students may feel that it is a cruel use of animals that trust their masters and do not expect to be ridden into a dangerous situation. Others may point out that horses have been used in wars for centuries. pp. 174–180)*

2. Why is driving the cab often as hard on the cab driver as it is on the horse? *(Inconsiderate passengers may, as they did to Jerry and Black Beauty, force the cab to wait for them in bad weather, thus endangering the health of both human and horse. Passengers may also make other demands on the cab driver and his horse, such as wanting them to work seven days a week. pp. 234–242)*

3. Beauty compares Jerry Barker to John Manly. In what ways are they alike? *(Both are kind and considerate of the horses' health. As a result, horses trust them to do the right thing and respond by doing their best. p. 181)*

4. In what incident does Jerry Barker show that his caring nature extends to all creatures, not just horses? *(He insists on taking a woman and her ailing child to the hospital even though she cannot afford to pay him. pp. 222–227)*

5. The Governor says, "Good Luck is rather particular who she rides with, and mostly prefers those who have got common sense and a good heart" (p. 188). What does he mean? Do you agree with him? If so, why? *(He probably means that people cannot depend on chance to provide them with what they need. They must use common sense to prepare themselves for future events. Also, if they treat others well, they can have some assurance that their kindness will be reciprocated. Answers will vary.)*

6. "My doctrine is this, that if we see cruelty or wrong that we have the power to stop, and do nothing, we make ourselves sharers in the guilt" (p. 205). In writing this, the author is undoubtedly expressing her own feelings. Do you think she lived up to her own guidelines? Explain. *(She did because, as the introductory piece on the first page explains, she devoted the last years of her life to educating the public with her book, writing even as she struggled to stay alive.)*

7. What event ends Jerry's cab driving career? *(He waits outside in the cold and sleet for his customers until after 1:00 a.m. He gets bronchitis and almost dies. The doctor tells him he should never drive a cab again. pp. 234–242)*

Supplementary Activities

1. Dramatic Reading: In groups, adapt one of the chapters in this part as a dramatic reading. Adopt voices that are suitable for your characters. Allow time for practice. If each group chooses a different chapter, or parts of different chapters, the presentation of the reading will provide a good summary of Part Three.

2. Writing: Choose a section of Beauty's narrative from Section 4 and rewrite it from a different point of view. For example, as he says on page 163, "No doubt a horse fair is a very amusing place to those who have nothing to lose; at any rate, there is plenty to see." You might, therefore, write from the point of view of one of those viewers.

3. Art: Select one or more passages from Chapter 32, "A Horse Fair," and illustrate them. Then caption your illustration with the passage it refers to.

4. Character Analysis: Begin a character analysis chart for Jerry Barker, a sensitive man with strong feelings about people and animals. Use the Feelings chart on page 14 of this guide.

Chapters 46–49, pp. 243–265

Beauty is worked hard by a less caring owner, and his health suffers. The next owner is even worse, so Beauty is sold once again. A kind gentleman and his grandson buy him to restore him to health. When some women take him on trial, he proves to be just what they need. The story comes full circle when their groom turns out to be none other than Joe Green, now grown up, who restores Black Beauty's name.

Vocabulary

persuasively (246)
detain (248)
indignities (251)
beseeching (252)
sufficiently (254)
speculation (259)
benefactor (259)
caresses (259)
extraordinary (261)
ventured (264)

Discussion Questions

1. What are the main reasons that working for the carter is so hard on Beauty? *(He overloads the cart and uses the bearing rein, which makes it hard for Beauty to pull any load, especially up a hill. pp. 245–249)*

2. What effect does the badly lighted stable have on Beauty's health? *(He becomes purblind, which means he is at least partially blind. p. 249)*

3. In what ways do children in this novel show that they can have more wisdom than the adults around them? *(A little girl tells her parents that the load is too heavy for the horse. A boy persuades his grandfather that they can rescue Beauty and restore his health. pp. 251–253, 257–260)*

4. Why does Black Beauty feel that any change from Nicholas Skinner must be an improvement? *(Skinner overworked him to the point that he fell from exhaustion. Black Beauty is hopeful that his next situation will be better. pp. 253–255)*

5. How does the advice Black Beauty's mother gave him long ago continue to help him even in his darkest moments? *(She told him to always do his best, so he tries to look as good as he can so that someone will buy him and take good care of him. p. 255)*

6. Why does Mr. Thoroughgood buy Black Beauty? *(He wants to make him young again. He realizes Black Beauty was once a great horse. pp. 257–260)*

7. Given that Black Beauty now has a good home and will not be sold again, why do you think he sometimes fancies that he is back at his first home, "standing with my old friends under the apple trees" (p. 265)? *(Students may respond that it was a happy time for him, and that he associates it with the present place, where he is once again being treated well.)*

8. How does Joe Green realize the new horse is Black Beauty? *(The horse has a white star on its forehead, a knot on its neck where Black Beauty was "bled" years before, and one white foot on the off side. p. 263)*

Supplementary Activities

1. Art: Working in groups, develop a list of rules for the humane treatment of pets. Illustrate a series of posters for each rule. If possible, display the posters throughout the school and/or in the school library.

2. Writing: Anna Sewell did not live to see the effects of her novel, yet her contributions to humane education may well have exceeded her fondest wishes. Research Sewell's life, then write a fitting dedication to memorialize her.

3. Art: Design a fitting monument in memory of Anna Sewell. Make your design one that actually serves the needs of the creatures the author cared so much about.

4. Science: Label a drawing or picture of a horse to identify the parts of its body, such as mane, forelock, withers, fetlock, hock, and hoof.

5. Writing: Predict what the rest of Black Beauty's life will be like under Joe Green's care. Write another chapter to the book telling about Black Beauty's life at his last home.

Post-reading Discussion Questions

1. Have you ever read a story similar to this one? What is that story about?

2. Who is your favorite character in the novel and why?

3. Who is the least likeable character in the novel? What makes him or her so unlikeable?

4. Think of all the characters you met, then choose one you would like to say something to. Who is it and what would you tell him or her?

5. What do you think is the most important event in the story? What other events happen as a result of it?

6. Do any of the characters, human or animal, remind you of people you know? In what way?

7. Would you recommend this book to a friend? Why or why not?

8. Did this novel change your ideas on the treatment of horses and other animals? If so, how?

9. Did any of the wishes you made for Black Beauty after reading Section 2 come true in Section 5? What were they?

Post-reading Extension Activities

Writing

1. Revisit the predictions you made about the novel. Write a description of which predictions were right and which were not.

2. Write a riddle that describes a character in the novel. Include clues that will help other students imagine this character. Describe how this character looks, feels, talks, and how other characters in the story treat him or her. Use the "Who Am I?" graphic on page 15 of this guide.

3. Research the penalties for cruelty to animals in your area. Do you think the penalties are too harsh? too lenient? Write a letter to a member of local government commenting on what you have learned.

Speaking/Acting

4. Imagine conducting a television interview with one of the characters in the novel. Invite a classmate to act out the interview with you.

5. Organize and stage a debate on a current issue regarding the treatment of animals. Possible topics might include rodeos, circus animals, and bullfighting.

Social Studies

6. According to the Web site of the Fund for Animals, the organization operates "the world famous Black Beauty Ranch in Murchison, Texas. The 1,620-acre refuge is home to many hundreds of animals—from chimpanzees to burros to elephants. Here, animals do not get harassed or harmed, but a helping hand and a loving home." Pretend you are an investigative reporter. Research the ranch and write an article using your findings. Use the graphic on page 16 of this guide.

Other Reading/Viewing

7. There are four movie versions of *Black Beauty*. Watch one of these versions on videotape or DVD. Then compare it with the book. How true is it to Sewell's book?

8. Read another book in which a horse is the main or one of the main characters. From what point of view is the book written? Does the author share Sewell's concerns about the treatment of horses? Which book do you prefer? Why?

Assessment for *Black Beauty*

Assessment is an ongoing process. The following nine items can be completed during the novel study. Once finished, the student and teacher will check the work. Points may be added to indicate the level of understanding.

Name _____ Date _____

Student   **Teacher**

_____   _____   1. Working in a small group, write five review questions for your assigned section. Participate in an oral review.

_____   _____   2. Compare your completed character charts and story map with members of a small group.

_____   _____   3. Write a short summary of the book, using at least ten vocabulary words.

_____   _____   4. As the teacher calls out certain character traits, write the name of the character in the book you think best matches each trait.

_____   _____   5. Write a two-line description of one of the characters, but omit the name. Exchange descriptions with a partner and identify the character s/he has described.

_____   _____   6. Set up an acrostic for Black Beauty. Write the letters of one of the qualities he revealed (courage, strength, adaptability) vertically on a piece of lined paper. Then write a series of sentences, each of which begins with one of the letters in the word and tells something about how Black Beauty developed the quality.

_____   _____   7. Correct all mistakes on quizzes.

_____   _____   8. Display or perform your Post-reading Extension project from page 25 of this guide on the assigned day.

_____   _____   9. Working with a small group, prepare a skit for one of the major scenes from the book. Perform it for the class and have your classmates guess which scene your group is performing.

Linking Novel Units® Lessons to National and State Reading Assessments

During the past several years, an increasing number of students have faced some form of state-mandated competency testing in reading. Many states now administer state-developed assessments to measure the skills and knowledge emphasized in their particular reading curriculum. The discussion questions and post-reading questions in this Novel Units® Teacher Guide make excellent open-ended comprehension questions and may be used throughout the daily lessons as practice activities. The rubric below provides important information for evaluating responses to open-ended comprehension questions. Teachers may also use scoring rubrics provided for their own state's competency test.

Please note: The Novel Units® Student Packet contains optional open-ended questions in a format similar to many national and state reading assessments

Scoring Rubric for Open-Ended Items

3-Exemplary	Thorough, complete ideas/information Clear organization throughout Logical reasoning/conclusions Thorough understanding of reading task Accurate, complete response
2-Sufficient	Many relevant ideas/pieces of information Clear organization throughout most of response Minor problems in logical reasoning/conclusions General understanding of reading task Generally accurate and complete response
1-Partially Sufficient	Minimally relevant ideas/information Obvious gaps in organization Obvious problems in logical reasoning/conclusions Minimal understanding of reading task Inaccuracies/incomplete response
0-Insufficient	Irrelevant ideas/information No coherent organization Major problems in logical reasoning/conclusions Little or no understanding of reading task Generally inaccurate/incomplete response

Notes